to our soulmates

Copyright ©1992 Marvel E. Harrison

Published by BRAT Publishing Corporation. All Rights Reserved.
No part of this book may be reproduced or transmitted in any form or by any means,
electronic or mechanical, including photocopying, recording, or by an information
storage and retrieval system without express permission in writing from the publisher.

Harrison, Marvel • Kellogg, Terry • Michaels, Greg

ISBN 1-880257-02-5

Printed in the United States of America

Other books offered by BRAT Publishing:

Finding Balance *12 Priorities For Interdependence and Joyful Living:*
Terry Kellogg & Marvel Harrison

Broken Toys Broken Dreams *Understanding and Healing Boundaries, Codependence,
Compulsion & Family Relationships:* Terry Kellogg

AttrACTIVE WOMEN *A Physical Fitness Approach To Emotional & Spiritual Well-Being:*
Marvel Harrison & Catharine Stewart-Roache

Butterfly Kisses *Little Intimacies For Sharing!* Harrison & Kellogg & Michaels

Hummingbird Words *Self Affirmations & Notes To Nurture By* Harrison & Kellogg & Michaels

Roots & Wings *Words For Growing A Family:* Harrison & Kellogg & Michaels

BRAT Publishing, Suite 225, 6 University Drive, Amherst, MA 01002
1-800-359-BRAT (2728)

butterfly kisses

little intimacies that can't be bought, sometimes noticed, sometimes not

marvel harrison   terry kellogg

illustrations by greg michaels

BRAT PUBLISHING

*h*ave you ever been very close to someone special and felt the wisp of an eyelash brush your cheek? you have been touched by the flutter of a butterfly kiss.

*b*utterfly kisses are gifts given and gifts received that build and maintain intimacy. some may not feel like gifts, a few might be scary, all involve taking risks. butterfly kisses are the precious moments in life we share and cherish with roommates, soulmates and playmates.

a book for anyone who hasn't given up completely and even they might secretly enjoy it!

*n*otice—especially little things

affirm all you can

cherish differences

let what is given be enough

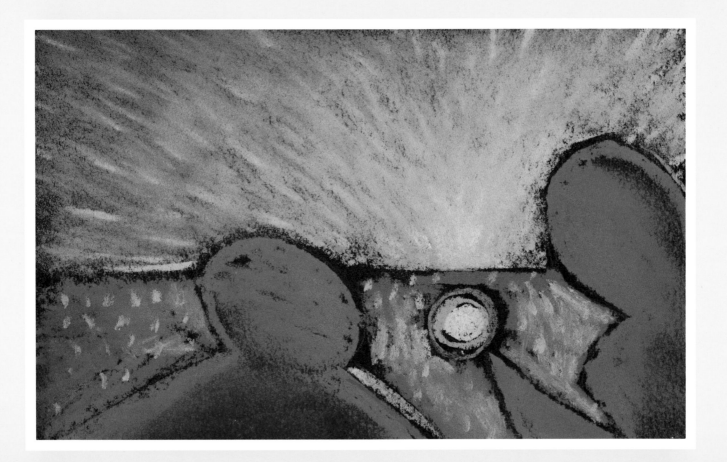

*d*ance alone

dance together

cherish childness

hold hands

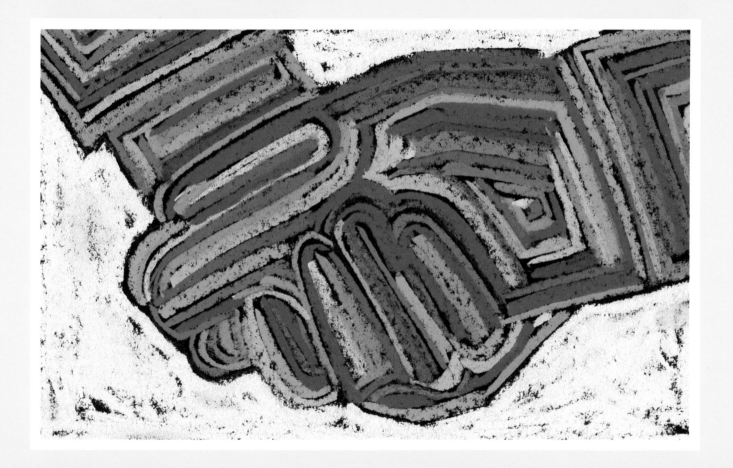

*t*alk even when it is difficult

write what you can't say

send flowers

do lunch

chat

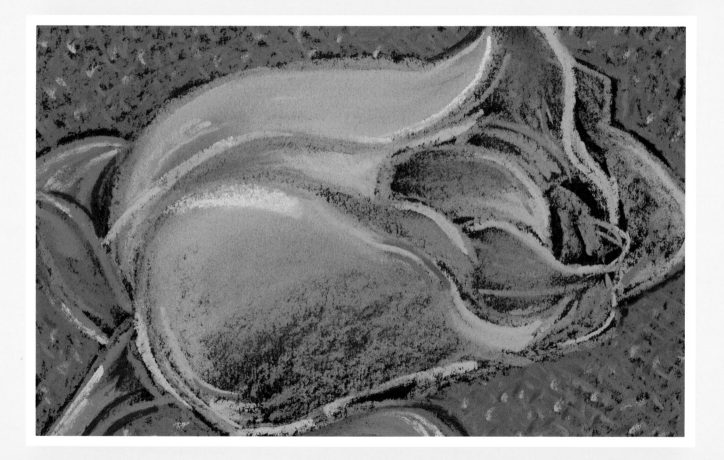

*k*now yourself

tell stories

record your history

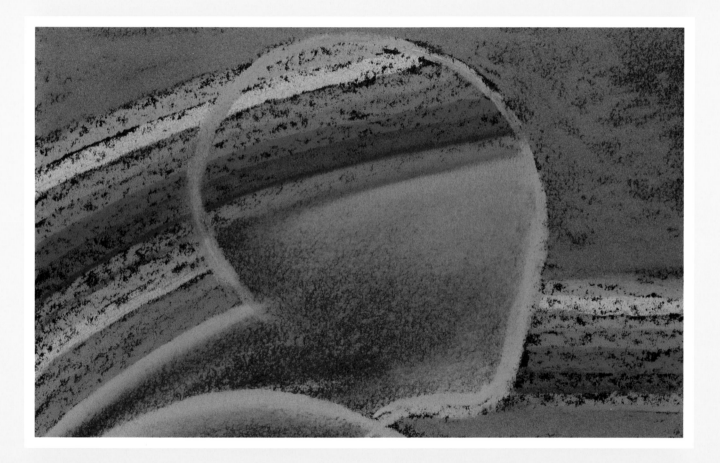

laugh, play and work

whisper, wink and giggle

snuggle

embrace your inner brat

*g*o slow, intimacy builds with time

be vulnerable

touch tears

grieve

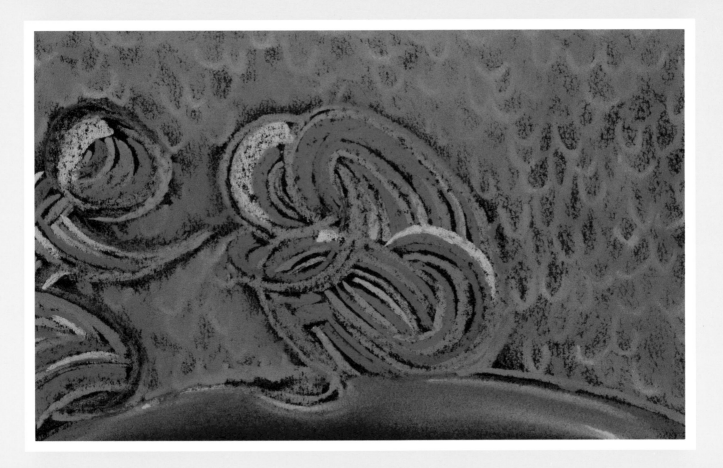

*d*on't compete

don't be cheap

don't be a creep

*g*ive up perfection

learn to fight

respect boundaries and privacy

allow silence

*S*hare beliefs and goals

walk in their shoes

sacrifice

support a cause

*t*ake a risk

make choices and mistakes

stay connected

forgive

remember real crises are rare

solve the problems you can

let some problems resolve themselves

let some problems remain problems

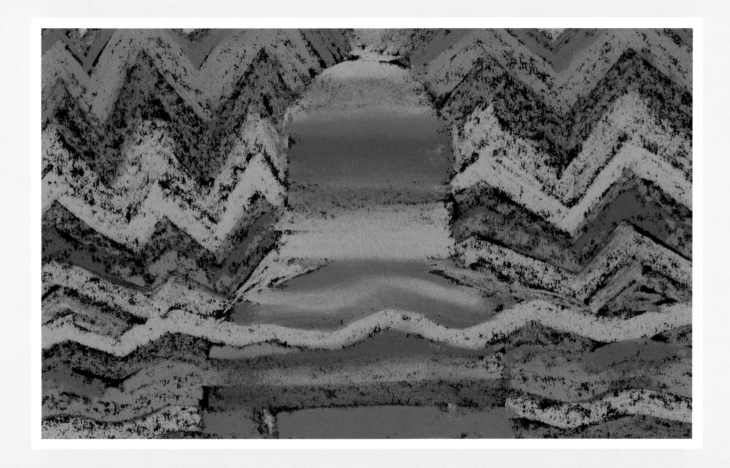

*b*end don't break

give up control

accept reality

*b*reak bread

make music

share candlelight

grow something

*t*ouch

talk about pleasuring

take time outs

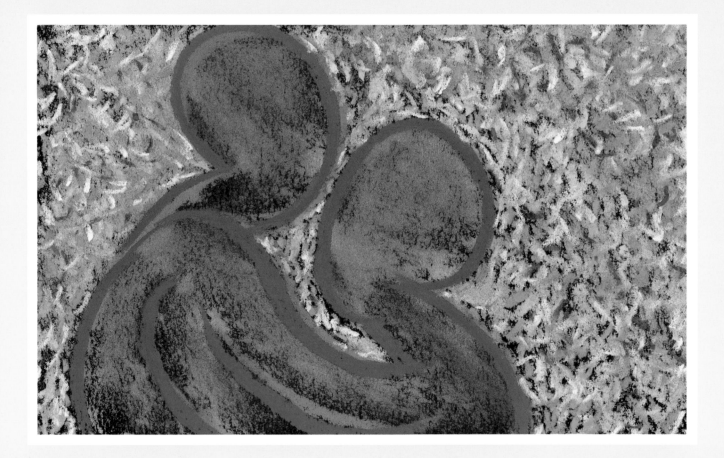

*i*nvest in self

enhance talents

look for joy within

network

*r*elish your body

share physical challenges

accept each other's pace

*C*omment gently

offer alternatives

show respect

*C*reate celebrations

ride ferris wheels, carousels and

roller coasters

believe in your magic

let your spirit soar

*r*espect rituals

notice creation

share gratitude

join in a spiritual journey

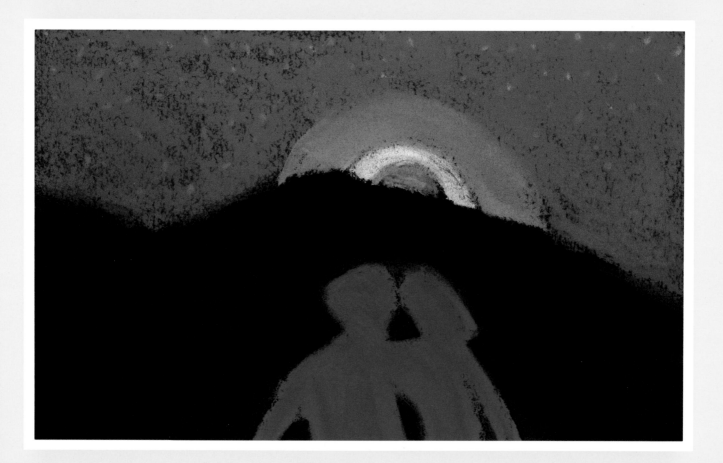

*a*nticipate rapids, waves

and still water

learn prayer and humor as postures

towards life and each other

Marvel Harrison, a native of Canada, is an avid runner, skier, canoeist and likes to play. She is a PhD candidate in Counseling Psychology, author, therapist and lecturer specializing in a gentle approach to self acceptance. Marvel's spirit and zest for life are easily felt by audiences everywhere.

Terry Kellogg is a parent, athlete, counselor and teacher. For twenty years he has been helping families with compulsive and addictive behaviors. Besides writing poetry, he is a wilderness enthusiast, an advocate for vulnerable groups and our planet. Terry is an entertaining, challenging, inspiring, and much sought after speaker.

Marvel and Terry are national education consultants to Baywood Hospital in Webster, TX and Program Advisors for Anacapa By The Sea Treatment Centers in Port Hueneme, CA.

Gregory Michaels is a full time dad and a free lance illustrator. His clever wit and sensitivity to children of all ages are apparent in his work and he has a terrific sense of humor to boot! Greg and his family make their home in the Rocky Mountains of Colorado.